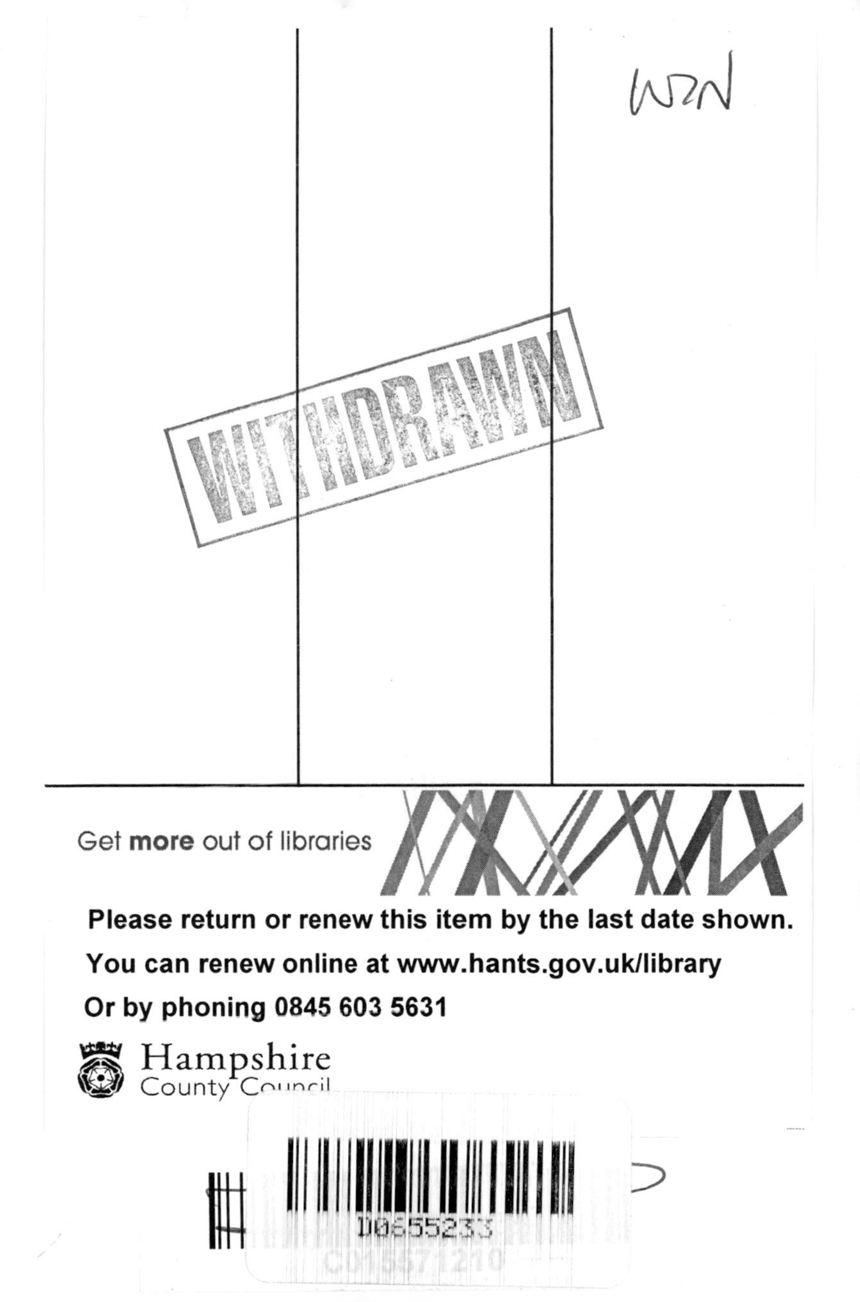
W2N
WITHDRAWN
Get more out of libraries
Please return or renew this item by the last date shown.
You can renew online at www.hants.gov.uk/library
Or by phoning 0845 603 5631
Hampshire
County Council
D0655233
C015571210

First published in the United Kingdom in 2013 by The Francis Frith Collection®

This edition published exclusively for Bradwell Books in 2013
For trade enquiries see: www.bradwellbooks.com or tel: 0800 834 920
978-1-84589-721-5



British Library Cataloguing in Publication Data

Flavours of Hampshire - Recipes
Compiled by Julia Skinner

The Francis Frith Collection
6 Oakley Business Park,
Wylye Road, Dinton,
Wiltshire SP3 5EU
Tel: +44 (0) 1722 716 376
Email: info@francisfrith.co.uk
www.francisfrith.com

Printed and bound in Malaysia
Contains material sourced from responsibly managed forests

Front Cover: **ANDOVER, BOYS IN THE HIGH STREET 1908** 60092p
Frontispeice: **RINGWOOD, THE MILLSTREAM 1900** 45027Ax
Contents: **ODIHAM, A DELIVERY BOY IN THE HIGH STREET 1908** 60088x

*The colour-tinting is for illustrative purposes only, and is not intended to be historically accurate*

AS WITH ANY HISTORICAL DATABASE, THE FRANCIS FRITH ARCHIVE IS CONSTANTLY BEING CORRECTED AND IMPROVED, AND THE PUBLISHERS WOULD WELCOME INFORMATION ON OMISSIONS OR INACCURACIES

# CONTENTS

# RECIPE

## Bean and Bacon Broth

Beans made up an important part of country people's diet in the past. This is an old Hampshire recipe for a hearty broth made with haricot beans. Either canned or dried beans can be used, but if you make this the authentic way with dried beans you need to soak them overnight in plenty of cold water before they can be used. Serves 4-6.

2 x 400g/14oz cans of haricot beans, drained to give 450g/ 1 lb weight of beans (or 225g/8oz dried haricot beans, soaked in cold water overnight then drained)
225g/8oz streaky bacon rashers, de-rinded
1 medium onion, peeled and finely chopped
2 sticks of celery, trimmed and cut into very thin slices
1.2 litres/2 pints chicken or vegetable stock
1 medium carrot, trimmed and cut into very thin slices
1 bay leaf
¼ teaspoonful freshly ground black pepper
Pinch ground cloves or allspice
1 x 400g/14oz can chopped tomatoes and their juice, or 225g/8oz fresh tomatoes, peeled and chopped into small pieces
Finely chopped fresh parsley, to garnish

A Hampshire folk belief in the past was that it was unlucky to give away or receive a gift of a parsley plant, as it meant someone in the recipient's family would die within the year. Instead, people always bought parsley plants from each other so the bad luck associated with giving the herb as a gift would be averted.

Cut the bacon into small pieces. Dry-fry them in their own fat in a frying pan until lightly browned, then remove to a large saucepan. Fry the onion and celery in the remaining fat for about 10 minutes until soft and transparent, then put it in the saucepan with the bacon, beans, sliced carrot and bay leaf. Add the stock, pepper and ground cloves or allspice – you should not need to add salt, as the bacon will make the broth salty. Bring to the boil, then reduce the heat and simmer for 1½-2 hours, until the beans are soft and tender (if using dried beans, allow the full 2 hours). Stir in the tomatoes and simmer for a further 30 minutes. Remove the bay leaf and serve with a garnish of finely chopped parsley, accompanied with hunks of crusty bread.

A tasty modern variation is to serve this with some finely-grated Parmesan cheese sprinkled on top, like a Hampshire version of Minestrone soup.

**STEEP, KETTLEBROOK 1898** 41362

## 'The ablest Herbalist in England'

The recipe on the opposite page commemorates the place of the Jerusalem artichoke in Hampshire's food history, as the county was the first place in England where it was grown. Originating from North America, it was introduced into English gardens and cuisine by the famous botanist and horticulturist John Goodyer (1592-1664), who was born in Alton and lived and worked in Hampshire all his life. In 1617 a friend in London sent Goodyer 'two small roots' of the plant as botanical curiosities, whilst he was working as the estate manager for Sir Thomas Bilson of the now-demolished West Mapledurham House near Buriton; Goodyer cultivated the plants in his garden and made Jerusalem artichokes popular.

In 1632 John Goodyer moved to Petersfield, where his house on The Spain area of the town still stands; it is now called 'Goodyers' and is marked with a commemorative plaque. During his lifetime John Goodyer had the reputation of being 'the ablest Herbalist now living in England'. In 1907 a protection order was discovered under the floorboards of his former home in Petersfield which was given to John Goodyer by the Royalist general Lord Hopton during the Civil War of the mid 17th century. Crops were failing at that time, and both Royalists and Parliamentarians needed Goodyer's botanical expertise to help avert a food crisis in the country. The protection order commanded all troops 'to defend and protect John Goodyer, his house, family, servants and estates'.

The Jerusalem artichoke (Helianthus tuberosis) is cultivated for its edible tubers, which can be roasted, boiled or mashed like potatoes to eat as a vegetable dish, or used to make a thick, creamy soup, as on the opposite page. The plant is a member of the sunflower family, and the 'Jerusalem' part of its name is probably an English corruption of its Italian name, 'Girasola articiocco', meaning the 'Sunflower artichoke' – the plant has no connection with the Holy Land.

# RECIPE

## Jerusalem Artichoke Soup

450g/1 lb Jerusalem artichoke tubers
2 sticks of celery, trimmed and sliced
1 medium onion, peeled and roughly chopped
1 tablespoonful cooking oil
3 level tablespoonfuls plain flour
600ml/1 pint chicken or vegetable stock
Salt and freshly ground black pepper
300ml/ ½ pint milk
Finely chopped fresh parsley to garnish

Wash the Jerusalem artichokes and scrub them well, but there is no need to peel them. Cut them into slices, then roughly chop them. Heat the oil in a large saucepan, add the chopped artichokes, celery and onion and cook over a medium heat, stirring frequently, for about 10 minutes. Stir in the flour and cook for a further minute, stirring continually. Gradually add the stock, just a little at a time at first as you blend it in, add salt to taste, then bring to the boil, stirring continually as the liquid thickens slightly. Reduce the heat, cover the pan with its lid and leave to simmer gently for about 45 minutes until the artichoke pieces are completely soft and tender, stirring occasionally so nothing sticks to the bottom of the pan. Remove from the heat and allow the soup to cool down a little. Process the soup through a blender or liquidizer until smooth, then return to the rinsed out pan. When ready to serve, add the milk and reheat, but do not allow the soup to boil. Season to taste with black pepper and extra salt if necessary, and serve sprinkled with finely chopped fresh parsley.

# RECIPE

## Watercress Soup

Hampshire is one of the UK's main areas for the production of watercress, which is widely grown in the area around Winchester. The restored and privately owned steam railway running between Alresford and Alton is known as 'The Watercress Line', as it was once a vital link for the local watercress industry. At one time, the line carried around 30 tons of watercress a week to the London markets from Alresford alone. Watercress is a super-food packed with nutrients, with a distinctive peppery and slightly bitter flavour. It can be eaten raw as a salad or in sandwiches and it is traditionally used in Hampshire to make a creamy sauce to accompany freshwater fish (see page 8). However, it is most famous for making a delicious soup. Serves 4-6.

50g/2oz butter
175g/6oz watercress (probably 2 bunches or packets)
1 medium onion, peeled and chopped
3 level tablespoonfuls plain flour
600ml/1 pint milk
450ml/ ¾ pint chicken or vegetable stock
6 tablespoonfuls single cream, and a little extra to garnish
Salt and pepper

Reserve a few sprigs of watercress to garnish the soup, then trim off any particularly coarse stalks and roughly chop the rest, both leaves and stalks. Melt the butter in a large pan, and gently fry the chopped onion for a few minutes until soft and transparent, then add the chopped watercress and cook for a further minute. Stir in the flour and cook for a further minute, stirring. Slowly blend in the milk, a little at a time, and then the stock, and season to taste with salt and pepper. Bring to the boil, stirring all the time as the soup thickens, then reduce the heat, cover the pan and simmer gently for 30 minutes. Remove from the heat and cool for a few minutes, then process through a blender or liquidizer until smooth. Before serving, add the 6 tablespoonfuls of cream and reheat gently, taking care not to allow the soup to boil. Check the seasoning and serve with a swirl of extra cream and a sprig of watercress leaves garnishing each helping.

GRAYSHOTT, WHITMORE VALE FARM, THE WELL 1915 67934x

# RECIPE

## Baked Trout with Watercress Sauce

Hampshire watercress is a natural combination with one of the county's other important foods – trout. Both are products of the wonderfully pure water that flows in the chalk streams and rivers of the county, and the Rivers Itchen and Test are particularly renowned for their trout. Watercress is used here to make a creamy sauce to accompany trout, but it is also very good with salmon. Serves 4.

4 trout, cleaned and gutted
300ml/ ½ pint water, or vegetable or fish stock
300ml/ ½ pint double cream
50g/2oz butter, cut into small pieces
1 bunch or packet of watercress
Salt and freshly ground black pepper

Pre-heat the oven to 180°C/350°F/Gas Mark 4. Place the fish closely together in a single layer in a greased, shallow ovenproof dish, laying them alternately head to tail to fit into the dish. Season, then pour the water or stock over the fish. Cover tightly with foil, and bake in the pre-heated oven for about 25 minutes, until the fish are tender. Remove the fish from the cooking liquor and use a sharp knife to peel off the skin. Keep the fish warm whilst you prepare the sauce. Reserve a few sprigs of watercress to garnish the finished dish, then trim off the long, coarse stalks and either chop the watercress leaves and remaining thinner stalks very finely by hand or put them through a food processor or liquidizer, adding a tablespoonful of the cream to help purée them if necessary. Boil the cream until it has reduced by half and thickened. Gradually whisk in the knobs of butter, a few at a time, then stir in the chopped watercress. If the sauce seems too thin, bring it back to the boil and reduce down for a minute or so. Serve at once, with the sauce poured over the warm, skinned trout, garnished with the reserved sprigs of watercress.

**CHILBOLTON, THE SEVEN STARS, TESTCOMBE (NOW THE MAYFLY) c1907** C227301

# RECIPE

## Crispy-Topped Baked Cod with Parsley Sauce

This is adapted from an old Hampshire recipe in which a whole cod was stuffed with a savoury breadcrumb mixture, then baked in the oven and served cut into slices. Individual portions of cod are used here instead, with the breadcrumb mixture forming a crispy topping, making this a quick and easy dish for modern cooks to prepare. Haddock portions can also be served this way. Serves 6.

6 cod steaks, cutlets or pieces of fillet, or frozen cod portions
75g/3oz fresh soft white breadcrumbs
50g/2oz shredded suet
Half a small onion, peeled and very finely chopped
1 dessertspoonful finely chopped fresh parsley
1 teaspoonful fresh chopped thyme (or ½ teaspoonful dried thyme)
Finely grated zest of one small unwaxed lemon
Salt and freshly ground black pepper
¼ teaspoonful freshly grated nutmeg
1 egg, beaten
50g/2oz butter

Pre-heat the oven to 180°C/350°F/Gas Mark 4. Mix together the breadcrumbs, suet, chopped onion, parsley, thyme, nutmeg and lemon zest. Season with salt and freshly ground black pepper, then stir in the beaten egg to form a moist, crumby mixture. Use some of the butter to liberally grease a shallow ovenproof dish and lay the cod portions in it in one layer. Spread the breadcrumb mixture over the fish, press down gently on the mixture to firm it up slightly, then dot small pieces of the remaining butter all over the topping. Bake in the pre-heated oven for 30-45 minutes (fish portions cooked from frozen will take longer to cook than fresh) until the fish is tender and the topping is crisp and golden, basting the topping occasionally with the buttery cooking juices in the dish.

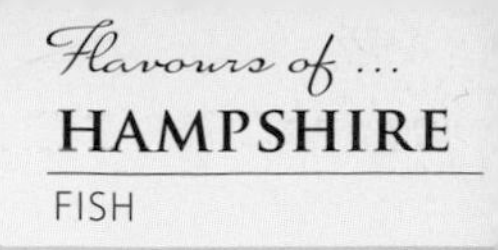

**SOUTHSEA, THE SEAFRONT 1892** 30018

Towards the end of the cooking time, make the parsley sauce.

25g/1oz butter
3 level tablespoonfuls plain flour
450g/ ¾ pint milk
Salt and freshly ground black pepper
2 heaped tablespoonfuls finely chopped fresh flat leaf parsley

Melt the butter in a saucepan. Add the flour and cook over a low heat for 2 minutes, stirring continually. Remove the pan from the heat and gradually blend in the milk. Return to the heat, bring to the boil and cook until the mixture thickens, stirring all the time. Reduce the heat and simmer gently for 2-3 minutes, then season to taste and stir in the chopped parsley. When the fish portions are cooked, serve them with boiled potatoes and peas and hand round the parsley sauce separately.

**ANDOVER, BOYS IN THE HIGH STREET**
**1908** 60092

POST
OFFICE

# RECIPE

## Hampshire Casserole

The unusual combination of beef, lamb and bacon in this dish is traditional to Hampshire.

350g/12oz beef braising or stewing steak, cut into cubes
225g/8oz shoulder or leg of lamb, cut into cubes
115g/4oz back bacon rashers, de-rinded and cut into small pieces
50g/2oz plain flour
Salt and freshly ground black pepper
Cooking oil for frying
2 onions, peeled and thinly sliced
2 carrots, sliced
675g/1½ lbs potatoes, peeled and thinly sliced
450ml/ ¾ pint beef stock

Put the flour in a bowl and season with salt and pepper. Roll the cubes of beef in the flour to coat them on all sides. Heat a tablespoonful of oil in a large frying pan and fry the cubes in batches to brown them on all sides, adding a little extra oil to the pan when necessary. Repeat with the lamb, keeping the two types of meat separate when browned. When all the meat is done, lightly fry the bacon pieces and remove from the pan, and then fry the sliced onions until soft and transparent but not browned. Pre-heat the oven to 180°C/350°F/Gas Mark 4. Put a layer of sliced potatoes in the bottom of a very large casserole dish and season. Cover with a layer of the beef, then continue with separate layers of the lamb, bacon, carrots, and onions, seasoning each layer as you go. Pour in the stock. Finish with a final layer of the remaining potato slices. Cover the casserole with its lid and cook in the oven for 2 hours. Remove the lid, brush the potato slices with a little oil, and return to the oven uncovered to bake for a further 30 minutes, until the potato slices on top are completely tender and browned at the edges.

**CRONDALL, THE FEATHERS 1906** 56350

# RECIPE

## Hampshire Farmhouse Flan

This savoury flan is a good way of using up a small amount of cooked chicken left over from a roast, and can be eaten either warm or cold.

225g/8oz plain wholemeal flour
50g/2oz butter
50g/2oz lard, refined vegetable fat or hard margarine for pastry-making
1 tablespoonful cooking oil
1 onion, peeled and finely chopped
1 garlic clove, crushed
225g/8oz cooked chicken, chopped into small pieces
75g/3oz watercress (about 1 bunch or packet)
Finely grated zest of half a small unwaxed lemon
2 eggs, lightly beaten
175ml/6 fl oz double cream
45ml/3 tablespoonfuls natural yogurt
¼ teaspoonful freshly grated nutmeg
50g/2oz Cheddar or Caerphilly cheese, grated
Salt and freshly ground black pepper
1 extra egg, beaten, to glaze the pastry strips to finish

First of all, make the pastry. Sift the flour and a pinch of salt into a mixing bowl. Cut the butter and fat or margarine into small pieces and rub it into the flour with your fingertips until the mixture resembles fine breadcrumbs. Use a round-bladed knife to stir in enough cold water to make a soft dough. Turn out the dough onto a lightly floured surface and knead it gently and briefly until it is smooth and elastic. Wrap the dough in cling film or a plastic bag and leave it in the fridge to 'rest' for 30 minutes.

Pre-heat the oven to 200°C/400°F/Gas Mark 6, and place a baking tray in the oven to heat up. Grease a round flan dish or tin about 22-24cms (9ins) in diameter, or a rectangular dish about 18 x 28cms (7 x 11ins), and line it with the rolled-out pastry, reserving the pastry trimmings. Line the pastry case with greaseproof paper and fill with baking beans or dry rice. Place the pastry case on the hot baking sheet in the pre-heated oven for 10 minutes, then remove the beans or rice and paper and cook for a further 5 minutes to dry out the pastry base.

Heat the oil in a large frying pan and cook the onion and garlic over a gently heat until soft and transparent, but not browned. Remove from the heat and leave to cool for a few minutes. Trim off the stalks from the watercress, and chop the leaves. Mix together the cooked onion and garlic, chopped watercress, chicken pieces and lemon zest, spoon it into the baked pastry case and spread evenly over the base. Beat together the 2 eggs, cream, yogurt, nutmeg and grated cheese. Season to taste with salt and freshly ground black pepper, then pour the mixture into the pastry case.

Roll out the pastry trimmings and cut into long, thin strips about 1cm (½ inch) wide, and long enough to cross over the flan dish or tin. Brush the strips with the extra beaten egg, then lay them in an open lattice pattern across the filling, pressing the ends firmly onto the pastry edge around the flan to fix and seal them.

Place the flan on the hot baking tray in the oven and bake for about 35 minutes, until the pastry is cooked, and the filling is firm to the touch and light golden-brown on top. Remove from the oven and leave for 15 minutes to cool a little and settle before serving the flan warm, or otherwise eat it cold.

Romsey prospered with the improved turnpike roads of the 18th and 19th centuries. The roads from Salisbury to Southampton and from Winchester to the west crossed the River Test there, and the coaching trade brought much business to the town's pubs and inns. At one time there were around 40 public houses in Romsey, giving it such a notorious reputation as a place of alcoholic over-indulgence that a local saying for a drunken man was that 'he must have been to Romsey'. Another saying was 'It's a straight road to Romsey, and a zig-zag back again'. A famous name in Romsey's past is the Strong & Co brewery, which was founded in the mid 19th century and endured until the early years of the 21st. At the company's peak Strong's bitter was served in pubs all over the south of England. Nowadays a celebrated Hampshire name in beer-drinking circles is the award-winning Ringwood Brewery on the extreme western edge of the county; founded in 1978, the excellent tipples produced by the Ringwood Brewery include Ringwood Best Bitter, Fortyniner and Old Thumper, all of which are available as bottled beers from their online shop: www.ringwoodbrewery.co.uk.

**ROMSEY, THE CORN EXCHANGE 1903** 49338

# RECIPE

## Beef Braised in Ringwood Beer

Use a Ringwood Brewery beer of your choice to make this beef stew with a rich gravy. Beer used in cooking should be of room heat, not chilled, and slightly flat, so open the bottle and decant it into a glass or jug a few minutes before using it in this recipe. If you're not able to use a Ringwood brew, use your own favourite beer in this recipe instead. Serves 4-6.

900g/2 lbs lean braising or stewing steak, cut into cubes
500ml/18fl oz (1 bottle) Ringwood Brewery beer of choice
1-2 tablespoonfuls cooking oil
3 medium-sized onions, peeled and cut into quarters
2 garlic cloves, crushed
1 rounded tablespoonful plain flour
1 teaspoonful dried mixed herbs
2 bay leaves
Salt and freshly ground black pepper

Pre-heat the oven to 150°C/300°F/Gas Mark 2. Heat one tablespoonful of the oil in a very large frying pan and fry the cubes of meat in small batches, a few pieces at a time, until they are well browned on all sides. As you brown the meat, remove it to a plate. When all the meat has been browned, add a little more oil to the pan if necessary, put in the sliced onions and fry for about five minutes until they are lightly browned at the edges, stirring them around as they cook. After that add the crushed garlic, let that cook for about 30 seconds, then turn the heat down, return the meat to the pan and sprinkle over the flour. Stir around with a wooden spoon until all the flour has been absorbed into the pan juices. Gradually stir in the beer, a little at a time, then turn up the heat and bring it to simmering point, stirring continually, until the sauce has thickened and is starting to bubble. Add the mixed herbs, bay leaves and salt and pepper. Pour it into a large casserole dish, cover with its lid and cook in the centre of the pre-heated oven for a full 2½ hours for the beer to mellow and become a tasty sauce. Serve with boiled, mashed or baked potatoes and seasonal vegetables.

On the western side of Hampshire is the New Forest. Now a National Park, it was created by William the Conqueror in the 11th century as a private hunting preserve for royalty. Although there is plenty of woodland in the New Forest, it also comprises stretches of heathland and grassy areas close-cropped by deer and the New Forest ponies that roam freely around the region. The Verderers are the officials who keep law and order in the Forest, meeting five times a year at the Verderers' Court in Lyndhurst. Under Forest Law in the Norman and medieval periods it was an offence for people living in the Royal Forests to hunt, wound or kill the king's deer, and their dogs had to be 'lawed' (or 'expediated') if they were over a certain size; this involved three claws being cut from the pad of each forefoot, which lamed the dog so it could not be used for unlawful hunting. In the Verderers' Hall at Lyndhurst is a 'dog stirrup' which was used to measure the dogs in the New Forest; it is 15cms (6 ins) in diameter, and only dogs small enough to pass through this device could roam the Forest without mutilation.

**LYNDHURST, HIGH STREET 1908** 60106

# RECIPE

## NEW FOREST VENISON CASSEROLE

Nowadays wild venison from the New Forest is legally available to anyone from local butchers or game dealers. Venison is a rich and well flavoured meat that is low in cholesterol and high in iron. It can sometimes be dry, but a good way of cooking it is in a pot roast, stew or casserole, to make sure it is tender and juicy.

1kg/2 lbs 4oz venison braising steak, cut into cubes
2 tablespoonfuls plain flour, seasoned
50g/2oz butter
2 tablespoonfuls oil
2 onions, peeled and thinly sliced
1 clove of garlic, peeled and finely chopped
600ml/1 pint stock
150ml/ ¼ pint red wine
1 tablespoonful tomato purée
225g/8oz carrots
115g/4oz mushrooms
2 dessertspoonfuls redcurrant jelly
Salt and freshly ground black pepper

Pre-heat the oven to 180°C/350°F/Gas Mark 4. Toss the cubes of venison in the seasoned flour so that all sides are covered. Melt half the butter and oil together in a flameproof casserole that has a tight-fitting lid. Fry the venison, a few cubes at a time, until all sides are browned. Put the browned meat to one side and keep warm. Melt the remaining butter and oil in the casserole, add the sliced onions and cook gently for about 10 minutes, until they are soft and transparent, then add the finely chopped garlic. Stir in the remaining seasoned flour and cook for 1-2 minutes, then add the tomato purée, and then the stock and the red wine, a little at a time, stirring continually. Increase the heat and bring the sauce to the boil, constantly stirring as the sauce thickens. Season to taste with salt and pepper, then add the sliced carrots and mushrooms and the browned venison pieces. Put the lid on the casserole and cook in the pre-heated oven for 1½-2 hours. Stir the redcurrant jelly into the casserole 10 minutes before serving.

# RECIPE

## Roast Pork – New Forest Style

An ancient common right claimed by people living in the New Forest is 'pannage', the right to turn pigs out into the Forest to feed on beech nuts (or 'mast') and acorns for around 60 days from September to November – the so-called 'Pannage Month'. Acorns fall from oak trees at this time and green acorns are poisonous to deer and ponies, but are excellent for fattening pigs. By the end of the Pannage Month the acorns have turned brown and are safe for deer and other creatures to eat, and pigs are then excluded from the Forest. This unusual recipe for roast pork comes from the New Forest, and was included by Elizabeth Ayrton and Theodora Fitzgibbon in their book 'Traditional British Cooking', first published in 1985. The joint of pork was originally roasted over shelled beech nuts which are found in great numbers in the New Forest; however, although beech nuts are edible they are rather bitter, and it is more usual nowadays to use a mixture of chopped walnuts and almonds or hazelnuts instead. Serves 4-6.

1 leg joint of pork, weighing 1.6-1.8kg (3½-4 lbs), with the skin scored with a sharp knife for crackling
3 level tablespoonfuls plain flour
Salt and freshly ground black pepper
115g/4oz shelled walnuts, finely chopped
75g/3oz blanched almonds or shelled hazelnuts, finely chopped
75g/3oz soft fresh brown breadcrumbs
25g/1oz butter for greasing the roasting dish

Pre-heat the oven to 200°C/400°F/Gas Mark 6. Mix the chopped nuts with the breadcrumbs and a good pinch of salt. Use the butter to grease a large roasting tin – put a particularly thick coating down the centre, and spoon the nut mixture on to this. Tidy and shape the mixture with your hands into a loose, flat layer about 1cm (½ inch) thick. Put the flour in a bowl, season with salt and pepper and rub it all over the pork joint. Place a roasting rack in the tin and set the joint on it, over the nut mixture. Do not put any fat or oil on the joint as there is enough fat in the pork to baste it whilst cooking. Roast in the pre-heated oven for 2 hours, basting occasionally with the fat in the tin.

Whilst the joint is cooking, roast the potatoes to accompany it in a separate tin below the pork. When the joint is cooked, transfer it to a warmed carving dish. Remove the nut mixture from the roasting tin and sprinkle some of it over the joint, pressing down on the top. Serve the remaining nut mixture as a side dish. Serve the pork with roast potatoes, vegetables, gravy and redcurrant jelly.

**NEW FOREST, PIGS NEAR BROOK c1955** N18004

# RECIPE

## HAMPSHIRE BACON PUDDING

Ham, bacon and pork feature strongly in traditional Hampshire cookery, and in fact the nickname for a Hampshire-born person is a 'Hampshire Hog'. Savoury suet puddings like this made an economical and filling meal for a large family in the past. This was originally wrapped in a pudding cloth and steamed for 3 hours, but the recipe is adapted here for the pudding to be baked in the oven which is quicker and gives a crispy finish to the pastry that modern families may prefer. However, it can be wrapped in greased and pleated kitchen foil and steamed if preferred. This was traditionally accompanied with mashed potatoes, mashed swede, carrots or parsnips and greens like cabbage or kale.

225g/8oz self-raising flour
Salt and freshly ground black pepper
115g/4oz shredded suet
350g/12oz lean bacon rashers, de-rinded and cut into small pieces
1 large or 2 medium onions, peeled and thinly sliced
25g/1oz butter, or one tablespoonful of cooking oil
1 dessertspoonful finely chopped fresh sage leaves
(or 1 teaspoonful dried sage)
A little milk, to glaze

Heat the butter or oil in a pan, add the sliced onion and fry gently until soft, then remove from the pan and put to one side. Fry the bacon pieces in the same pan until cooked through, return the onion to the pan and season well with freshly ground black pepper. Leave to cool whilst you make the pastry. Sieve the flour into a bowl, season with salt and pepper and add the suet. Mix with enough cold water to form a soft dough. Roll out the dough quite thinly on a floured surface to form a rectangle, spread with the bacon and onion mixture, leaving a margin around the edges, and sprinkle over the chopped sage. Dampen the edges of the dough and roll it up like a Swiss roll. Pinch the edge and ends to seal them. Place on a greased baking sheet with the join side underneath, and brush with milk to glaze. Bake in a pre-heated oven at 200°C/400°F/Gas Mark 6 for 30-40 minutes, until the pastry is crusty and golden brown. Serve cut into thick slices.

**BASINGSTOKE, CHURCH STREET 1904** 52129

# RECIPE

## KIDNEYS IN ONIONS

Southampton stands at the head of Southampton Water, the wide tidal estuary and confluence of two of Hampshire's great rivers, the Test and the Itchen, both of which empty into the sea at this point. Cloth and wool were particularly important exports from medieval Southampton's busy port, and in more recent times this important maritime centre became the home port of many great luxury passenger liners, including the ill-fated 'Titanic', the 'Queen Mary', Queen Elizabeth' and 'Queen Elizabeth II'. This dish used to be a speciality of Southampton inns, where it was a great favourite with sailors on shore leave. The kidney-stuffed onions were prepared in large trays and cooked in the inns' bread ovens before being served to the sailors for their supper. Those jolly Jack Tars of old liked to pour a dash of rum into the onion gravy before eating it, but you can use red wine instead if you prefer. This dish is traditionally eaten like soup, using a spoon – the kidneys are very soft when cooked. It may seem rather fiddly to prepare but is very tasty and well worth the effort, and after it goes in the oven it cooks itself. It makes an ideal supper dish for a cold winter's day. This amount serves 2-4 people depending on appetite, but can easily be increased for more – just add more stock and another tablespoonful of rum or wine if making this with extra onions.

4 large onions
4 lamb kidneys, trimmed and cored
25g/1oz butter
Salt and freshly ground black pepper
450ml/ ¾ pint good lamb or beef stock
50ml/3 tablespoonfuls rum or red wine, as preferred
Finely chopped fresh parsley to garnish
Hot buttered toast, to serve

Pre-heat the oven to 180°C/350°F/Gas Mark 4.

Peel the skin off the onions but leave them whole. Cut the top off each onion and put the pieces to one side to use later as lids. Use a teaspoon to scoop and scrape out the centre of each onion to make a hollow large enough to hold a kidney, reserving the onion scrapings to use later.

Bring a large pan of water to a fast boil, add the onions and parboil them for 8-10 minutes, until they begin to soften. Drain the onions and stand them open side up in an ovenproof dish or casserole deep enough to hold the onions with its cover on. Season the onions inside and out with salt and pepper.

Melt the butter in a pan, add the kidneys and cook them for a few minutes on each side. Season with salt and pepper. Fit a kidney inside the hollow of each onion, then cover the onions with their lids. Roughly chop the onion scrapings and scatter them around the stuffed onions in the dish. Pour in the juices from the pan the kidneys were cooked in, then add the stock. Cover the dish with its lid and cook in the pre-heated oven for 1½ hours. Remove the dish from the oven and stir the rum or red wine into the cooking liquid. Replace the lid of the dish, return to the oven and cook for a further 30 minutes.

Serve the onions in individual soup bowls with the onion gravy spooned over them, sprinkled with finely chopped parsley and accompanied with hot buttered toast.

**SOUTHAMPTON, BARGATE**
**1908** 60428

Flavours of ...
HAMPSHIRE
MEAT, POULTRY & GAME

# RECIPE

## ROASTED PUMPKIN

The fertile soil of Hampshire means that farming of all types is carried out in the county. The wide variety of crops grown includes soft fruit, cereal crops and various root vegetables, as well as pumpkins. A popular event in the county's calendar is the annual Pumpkin Festival in October at Queen Victoria Country Park at Netley, near Southampton. A highlight of the festival is the extreme pumpkin-growing competition, when the heaviest monster vegetable is declared the festival's champion. You won't need a giant pumpkin for this recipe though! Pumpkin makes a delicious vegetable dish with a sweet flavour when simply roasted in the oven like this, and is a good way of using up the pumpkin flesh left over from making Halloween lanterns at the end of October. Serves 4–6.

1 medium pumpkin, about 20-24cms (8-9ins) in diameter
3 tablespoonfuls olive oil
A handful of fresh sage leaves (left whole, not chopped)
Salt and freshly ground black pepper
Half a teaspoonful freshly grated nutmeg

Pre-heat the oven to 200°C/400°F/Gas Mark 6.

Peel the pumpkin, de-seed it and cut the flesh into chunks or slices about 4cms (1½ ins) thick. Put the pumpkin pieces into a large roasting tin with 2 tablespoonfuls of the olive oil, season with salt and pepper, and toss the pieces in the oil so that all the sides are coated. Roast the pumpkin in the pre-heated oven for 35-40 minutes, or until the pieces are golden and tender when tested with a skewer or the point of a sharp knife, turning them once during the cooking time. Add the sage leaves to the tin for the last 5 minutes of the cooking time. Remove the tin from the oven, drizzle the rest of the olive oil over the pumpkin pieces and grate a little nutmeg over them. Serve straight away.

**EVERSLEY, THE WHITE HART, THE KNIFESHARPENER 1906** 57011

**PORTSMOUTH, THE HARBOUR AND HMS 'VICTORY' 1898** 42705

A key seafaring city and naval port since early times, Portsmouth evolved over the years into southern England's largest and most important naval base. Its first ship repair facilities were probably built in the late 12th or early 13th century, and in the 16th century the Tudor kings, Henry VII and Henry VIII, constructed the first dry dock in the world there. By the end of the 17th century Portsmouth was the most strongly defended place in the country, and the leading naval dockyard; in later years it played a key role in the defence of the British Empire, and became synonymous with the navy. The nickname of both the city of Portsmouth and its football club is 'Pompey', but no one is exactly sure why. The most plausible reason relates to the story of the Portsmouth-based sailors who in 1781 scaled Pompey's pillar in Alexandria in Egypt and toasted their success from the top with punch. Their efforts earned them the nickname 'the Pompey Boys'.

# RECIPE

## Broccoli and Leek Tart

Market gardening has been important in the southern part of Hampshire for many years, and in the 19th century vast quantities of cabbages and other vegetables were brought to the Portsmouth markets to supply the dockyards and several hospitals serving the area. It was said at this time that Portsea Island produced the best broccoli in the kingdom!

175g/6oz plain flour, sifted
115g/4oz butter or margarine
25g/1oz tasty cheese of choice, grated
2 small leeks, trimmed and very thinly sliced
75g/3oz small broccoli florets
150ml/ ¼ pint milk
2 eggs, beaten
30ml/2 tablespoonfuls double cream
A pinch of ground mace
Salt and freshly ground black pepper
15g/ ½ oz flaked almonds, lightly toasted, to garnish

Blend the flour, butter and cheese together either in a food processor or by hand until the mixture resembles fine breadcrumbs. Add salt to taste. Stir in 4-6 tablespoonfuls of cold water, mix and knead to form into a ball of pastry, then chill the pastry in the fridge for about 15 minutes.

Preheat the oven to 190°C/375°F/Gas Mark 5. Roll out the pastry on a floured surface and use it to line a flan dish or tin about 20-22cms (8-9ins) in diameter. Line the pastry case with greaseproof paper and fill with baking beans. Bake the pastry case for 15 minutes, then remove the beans and paper and cook for a further 5 minutes to dry out the base.

Place the milk in a saucepan and bring to the boil, then add the vegetables, reduce the heat and simmer gently for 2-3 minutes. Strain the milk into a bowl and whisk in the eggs, mace, seasoning and cream. Arrange the drained vegetables in the pastry case and pour the egg mixture over them. Bake for 20 minutes, or until the filling is just firm to the touch. Sprinkle with the toasted almonds and leave for 15 minutes to cool a little and settle before serving the tart warm, or otherwise eat it cold.

# RECIPE

## NELSON SLICES

This recipe is named after Britain's naval hero of the Napoleonic Wars, Admiral Lord Nelson (1758–1805), who left England for the last time when he sailed out of Portsmouth on his flagship HMS 'Victory' on September 14th 1805. A few weeks later he died on board the 'Victory' during his greatest triumph of the Battle of Trafalgar against a combined French and Spanish fleet off the coast of Spain, shot by an enemy sniper. For many years the 'Victory' was moored in Portsmouth harbour, as seen in the background of the photograph on page 32, but in 1922 she was towed to her current berth in Portsmouth Historic Dockyard, where she is still the flagship of the Commander-in-Chief, Naval Home Command, the oldest naval ship in the world still in commission, and Portsmouth's most popular visitor attraction. A visit to the ship gives a fascinating glimpse of what life was like for the 828 crew on board the ship in Nelson's time, as well as for Nelson himself.

Perhaps this version of bread pudding was named after Nelson because of the addition of rum, reminiscent of the daily tot of rum issued to sailors in the Royal Navy from 1665 until 1970. Alternatively, it may refer to the cask of rum in which Nelson's body was preserved on the voyage home from the battle before his state funeral in St Paul's Cathedral in London.

This is a good way of using up old bread past its best. It can be eaten either hot as a pudding, cut into slices and served with custard or cream, or cold as thick, filling slabs of cake. The mixed peel can be replaced with an extra 50g/2oz of dried fruit if you like, and the rum can be omitted if you prefer.

225g/8oz old bread, white or brown, including the crusts (6-8 slices)
300ml/ ½ pint milk
1 dessert apple
350g/12oz mixed dried fruit – currants, raisins, sultanas
50g/2oz finely chopped mixed peel
115g/4oz soft dark brown sugar
2 tablespoonfuls good quality orange marmalade
50g/2oz self-raising flour
2 eggs, beaten
1 teaspoonful ground cinnamon
2 teaspoonfuls ground mixed spice
1-2 tablespoonfuls dark rum, to taste
115g/4oz butter

Pre-heat the oven to 150°C/300°F/Gas Mark 2. Grease a wide, shallow ovenproof dish or baking or roasting tin about 28 x 22cms (11 x 9ins) or equivalent. Break the bread (including the crusts) into small pieces, place in a mixing bowl and pour the milk over. Stir it around a bit so it all gets moistened (it may seem very dry, but do not add more milk) then leave to soak for 1 hour. When soaked, beat well with a fork to break up any lumps and form a smooth, damp crumby mixture (this may take a few minutes). Peel and core the apple and grate it into the bread mixture. Add the dried fruit and peel, the sugar, marmalade, flour, beaten eggs, cinnamon, mixed spice and the rum, and mix it all together thoroughly. Melt the butter in a pan over a gentle heat, then pour three-quarters of it into the mixture and beat it in well. Spread the mixture evenly into the prepared dish or tin, then drizzle the remaining melted butter over the surface. Bake in the pre-heated oven for 1½ hours, then increase the oven temperature to 180°C/350°F/Gas Mark 4, and bake for a further 30 minutes. This can then either be eaten hot from the oven as a pudding, or cold as a cake – for the latter, dredge the surface liberally with sugar when you remove it from the oven then leave to cool before cutting it into square slices.

'DOUBTLESS GOD COULD HAVE MADE A BETTER BERRY, BUT DOUBTLESS GOD NEVER DID.'

*On the strawberry – William Butler (1535–1618)*

Whereabouts in Hampshire can you find a pub named after a strawberry? The answer is at Locks Heath, west of Fareham, where the Sir Joseph Paxton pub in Hunts Pond Road is not only named after the famous 19th-century botanist but also commemorates the variety of strawberry he developed. From the 1860s until the mid 20th century there was an important strawberry-growing industry around Locks Heath. The Sir Joseph Paxton strawberry was particularly popular in the area, and was so widely grown that the itinerant workers employed to harvest the fruit were nicknamed 'Joe pickers'.

Locks Heath was formed after Titchfield Common was enclosed in the 1860s and its land was sold off in small plots. It was cultivated by market gardeners who discovered the soil was ideal for strawberry growing, as its high gravel content and poor moisture-retaining properties meant it warmed up quickly in spring, causing the local crop to ripen earlier than in other places. Getting the fruit to market early in the year meant high prices and bigger profits, so the local strawberry industry was boosted tremendously by the opening of Swanwick Railway Station in 1887. When the strawberries were ripe, itinerant labourers and Gypsies descended upon the fruit fields to help local people gather the harvest. Local schools arranged early summer holidays so their pupils could help too, and these 'strawberry holidays' became a feature of the area. The strawberries were transported by pony and donkey carts to the railway station to be loaded onto trains known as 'Strawberry Specials'. In 1928, 1,287,925 baskets of strawberries left Swanwick Railway Station for the markets of London and the provinces.

By the 1930s the soil would no longer yield the crops because of disease and over-cultivation, then restrictions on fruit production during the Second World War hastened the decline of strawberry growing. The local industry never recovered after the war, but a link with the past still continues with the strawberry fields off Titchfield Road, where in late spring and early summer you can pick your own strawberries and hark back to the days when Fareham was the pick of the crop.

# RECIPE

## Strawberry Fool

This recipe celebrates the proud place of strawberries in Hampshire's food history by using them to make a creamy fool. Make this dessert on the day you want to eat it and chill it well before serving, to intensify the delicious flavour of the fruit. Serves 6.

450g/1 lb fresh strawberries, hulled
115g/4oz caster sugar
1 teaspoonful lemon juice
300ml/ ½ pint double or whipping cream
2 egg whites

Reserve a few strawberries to decorate the finished dish, then chop the remaining berries into a food processor or liquidizer, add the lemon juice and sugar and process to a purée –
don't over-process it, as it's nice to have a few small fruity bits in the fool. (Alternatively, mash the fruit with a fork or potato masher.)

Whip the cream until it is thick and soft, then use a large metal spoon to fold it into the strawberry purée. Whisk the egg whites until they are stiff and soft peaks form, and fold them into the fool as well, mixing them in gently but thoroughly.

Pour the mixture into a pretty serving dish, and decorate with the whole strawberries, or slice them if preferred. Cover the dish with cling film and leave the fool to chill and set in the fridge for several hours before serving.

# RECIPE

## Hampshire Tart

This is an open tart with an egg custard topping over a layer of strawberry jam. It can be eaten hot or cold. Serves 4.

175g/6oz shortcrust pastry (if making your own, use 115g/4oz flour to 50g/2oz fat)
Strawberry jam
75g/3oz caster sugar
75g/3oz butter, melted, then left to cool slightly
2 eggs, and 2 additional egg yolks

Pre-heat the oven to 180°C/350°F/Gas Mark 4.
Place a baking tray in the oven to heat up.

Grease a small flan or pie dish or tin about 18cms (7ins) in diameter. Line it with the rolled out pastry and prick all over the base with a fork. Spread a layer of jam across the base.

Beat together the sugar, melted butter, eggs and egg yolks, and spread the mixture over the jam. Place the dish on the hot baking tray in the oven (this helps the pastry base to cook through) and bake for about 30 minutes, until the filling is risen and just firm to the touch. Remove from the oven and leave for a few minutes for the filling to settle and firm up before serving hot, or leave to cool completely and eat cold.

# RECIPE

## HAMPSHIRE SIX-CUP PUDDING

This steamed pudding is like a lighter, spongier version of Christmas Pudding, and is a good way of using up old bread past its best. It got its name because its six main ingredients were originally measured in cupfuls, although the Hampshire pudding uses more sugar than versions found elsewhere.

115g/4oz self-raising flour
115g/4oz soft breadcrumbs (white or brown)
115g/4oz suet
115g/4oz mixed raisins, sultanas and currants
175g/6oz dark or light soft brown sugar
1 teaspoonful mixed spice
300ml/ ½ pint milk
1 teaspoonful bicarbonate of soda
1 egg, beaten

Mix all the dry ingredients together except the bicarbonate of soda. Warm the milk to lukewarm and dissolve the bicarbonate of soda in it. Leave to cool for a few minutes, then add the milk to the other ingredients, together with the beaten egg, and mix well. Grease a pudding basin of 900ml-1.2 litre (1-2 pint) capacity and fill it with the mixture. Cover the basin with a lid of pleated kitchen foil (to allow room for expansion during cooking), buttered on the pudding side, then a further piece of pleated foil, and tie down firmly with string. Place the basin in the top half of a steamer or a large saucepan filled with boiling water to a third of the way up its side, cover the pan with its lid and steam the pudding for 3 hours, adding more boiling water to the pan when necessary to stop it boiling dry. Lift the basin from the pan and leave the pudding to settle in the basin for 5 minutes. Remove the foil lid, run a knife around the inside of the basin to loosen the pudding, then invert it onto a warmed serving dish. Serve hot with custard or cream.

**WINCHESTER, THE BUTTERCROSS 1899** 43677

The county town of Hampshire is the historic city of Winchester. At the time of the Roman invasion of Britain in AD43 the Winchester area was a stronghold of the Iron Age tribe known as the Belgae. The Romans named their market town beside the River Itchen after them, calling it 'Venta Belgarum', or 'the town of the Belgae'. In later centuries the Hampshire area was settled by Jutes and Saxons who called the old Roman town at Winchester a 'ceaster', and changed its name to 'Venta Ceaster'. Over time this became 'Wintancaester', and eventually 'Winchester', the capital of the Anglo-Saxon kingdom of Wessex and later of Anglo-Saxon England. This view shows the restored medieval Buttercross that stands in Winchester's High Street, so-called because in past times local women used to sell butter from its steps.

# RECIPE

## WINCHESTER PUDDING

This is like a rich, fruited rice pudding and is based on a recipe published in the 'Harmworth's Self-Educator' magazine in 1906. The pudding in the original recipe had to be steamed for 2-3 hours, but this version has been adapted for baking in the oven, so is much quicker to make. The mixed peel in the pudding may not be to modern tastes so can be omitted if preferred, or replaced with extra raisins.

75g/3oz short grain pudding rice
600ml/1 pint whole (full fat) milk
115g/4oz raisins
75g/3oz mixed peel (optional)
50g/2oz suet
50g/2oz caster sugar
Grated zest of one small unwaxed lemon
½ teaspoonful grated nutmeg
2 eggs, beaten

Put the milk and pudding rice into a saucepan and gently bring to the boil, stirring occasionally so the rice doesn't stick to the bottom of the pan. Reduce the heat, cover the pan with its lid and leave to cook over a very low simmer for 30-45 minutes, stirring occasionally, until the rice is soft and tender and has absorbed nearly all the milk. Remove from the heat and leave to cool for a few minutes.

Pre-heat the oven to 180°C/350°F/Gas Mark 4 and grease a 1.2 litre/2 pint ovenproof dish.

Mix together the raisins, peel (if using), suet, caster sugar, lemon zest and nutmeg. Stir into the rice and milk mixture, then beat in the eggs until it is all well combined. Turn the mixture into the prepared dish and bake in the pre-heated oven for 25-30 minutes, until the pudding is set and golden brown on top. Serve with some single cream poured over.

The pride of Winchester is its magnificent cathedral. In medieval times pilgrims came there from all over Europe to visit the shrine of St Swithun, a former Bishop of Winchester who was known for his lack of pomp and ostentation. After he died in AD862 he was buried in the churchyard as he had requested, saying he wanted the rain to fall on him, but over a century later his remains were moved from their original resting-place to his shrine inside the cathedral. After this was done, there was a period of rain that lasted 40 days; it was believed that the saint was displeased with his bones being moved and had protested by 'weeping', which gave rise to the saying that if it rains on St Swithun's Day (July 15th), it will continue to rain for the next 40 days. Another popular belief was that if it rained on St Swithun's Day the saint was blessing the apples in the orchards, and there would be a good harvest.

**WINCHESTER, THE CATHEDRAL 1911** 63722

# RECIPE

## Friar's Omelette

Apples feature in this old Hampshire pudding recipe, which is nothing like an omelette despite its traditional name. It is best to prepare the apple pulp for this dish by baking the apples in the oven, rather than stewing them in water, as this results in a drier pulp and gives a much better result.

450g/1 lb cooking apples
50g/2oz caster sugar, plus more to finish
50g/2oz butter
2 eggs
Grated zest of one small unwaxed lemon
¼ teaspoonful ground cinnamon, plus a little more to finish
115g/4oz fresh soft white breadcrumbs

Heat the oven to 200°C/400°F/Gas Mark 6. Remove the cores from the apples, but do not peel them. Use a sharp knife to score a line around the outside of each apple, then stand them in an ovenproof dish in 2 tablespoonfuls of water and bake in the pre-heated oven for 40 minutes until the apples are tender. Remove them from the oven and reduce the oven temperature to 180°C/350°F/Gas Mark 4. Remove the skins from the apples and mash the pulp with a fork to form a purée. Melt half the butter in a saucepan, then leave it to cool for a few minutes. Beat together the eggs and sugar, then stir in the apple pulp, lemon zest, cinnamon and melted butter, and mix it all together well. Grease an ovenproof dish about 1.2 litres (2 pints) in capacity and spread half the breadcrumbs over its base. Pour over the apple mixture and spread it evenly, then cover with the rest of the breadcrumbs. Sprinkle the topping with a little more cinnamon, then dot very small pieces of the remaining butter all over it. Bake just below the centre of the pre-heated oven at the reduced temperature for 45-50 minutes, until the pudding is firm and set and the topping is golden brown and crispy. Remove from the oven and sprinkle extra sugar over the top before serving with cream or custard.

# RECIPE

## Brown Bread and Honey Ice-Cream

Winchester College in Winchester is one of the oldest public schools in England. It was founded in 1382 by William of Wykeham, who was born the son of a serf in 1324 at Wickham in Hampshire, south of Bishop's Waltham, and rose to become Bishop of Winchester from 1367 to 1404 and also Chancellor of England. The original purpose of the school was to prepare 70 poor scholars for entry to New College, Oxford, which William of Wykeham also founded, and then for the priesthood. One of William's sayings, 'Manners maketh Man', is the motto of both Winchester College and New College, Oxford. Winchester College was the original home of Brown Bread and Honey Ice-Cream, where for many years it was made to a closely guarded secret recipe and sold in the Tuck Shop.

300ml/ ½ pint double cream
3 tablespoonfuls of thick honey
75g/3oz wholemeal bread, with the crusts removed
1 tablespoonful of orange juice
25g/1oz caster sugar

Cut the bread into slices, and place them on a baking tray in a low oven for about 20 minutes, or until they start to harden. Do not allow the bread to dry out too much. Lightly whip the cream and sugar together and place the mixture in the freezer for about 30 minutes. Crumble the bread in a blender or food processor to make breadcrumbs, and put them in a small bowl. Melt the honey over a gentle heat, and mix in the orange juice. Pour the honey mixture over the breadcrumbs, then mix the sweetened breadcrumb mix with the semi-frozen cream, combining it all together well. Freeze for a further 2 hours before serving. As this mixture will not form ice crystals it will not require further whipping. If using an ice-cream maker, sprinkle the breadcrumb mixture into the cream mix about halfway through the process.

# RECIPE

## GOOSEBERRY STIRABOUT

This batter pudding can also be made with blackberries, blueberries, plums, cherries, chopped apples or rhubarb, cut into pieces about 2.5cms (1 inch) long. Serves 4.

115g/4oz plain flour
50g/2oz butter or margarine
50g/2oz caster sugar
1 egg, beaten into 5 tablespoonfuls of milk (75ml/2½ fl oz)
225g/8oz gooseberries, topped and tailed (or alternative fruit)
Sugar or golden syrup to serve

Pre-heat the oven to 220°C/425°F/Gas Mark 7. Grease an ovenproof dish or tin about 20cms (8ins) square or equivalent. Rub the fat into the flour, stir in the sugar and gradually blend in the beaten egg and milk to form a stiff batter. Mix in the fruit, pour into the dish and bake for about 30 minutes, until risen and golden. Serve piping hot, cut into slices, sprinkled with sugar or with golden syrup poured over.

**FARNBOROUGH, LYNCHFORD ROAD**
**1905** 53259

# RECIPE

## 'A Good Apple Pie'

The novelist Jane Austen was born in 1775 in the Hampshire village of Steventon near Basingstoke, where her father was the rector, and she lived in the county all her life except for a few years in Bath. A short distance south of Alton is Chawton, where she lived from 1809 until her death in 1817 and where she wrote 'Mansfield Park', 'Emma' and 'Persuasion'. Her former home at Chawton is now the Jane Austen House Museum. Jane Austen was very partial to apple pie, and in 1815 she wrote in a letter to her sister that 'Good Apple Pies are a considerable part of our domestic happiness'.

For the pastry:
225g/8oz plain flour
50g/2oz butter
50g/2oz lard, refined vegetable fat or hard margarine for pastry-making
Pinch of salt
1 rounded dessertspoonful caster sugar
2-3 tablespoonfuls cold water

To finish:
1 egg, beaten
A little extra caster sugar

For the filling:
900g/2 lbs Bramley apples (unprepared weight)
115g/4oz white or soft brown sugar (or a little more, to taste)
50g/2oz plain flour
Half a teaspoonful ground cinnamon
50g/2oz sultanas (optional)
Juice of half a lemon
25g/1oz butter, cut into pieces

First of all, make the pastry. Sift the flour and salt into a mixing bowl, and stir in the dessertspoonful of sugar. Cut the butter and fat or margarine into small pieces and rub it into the flour with your fingertips until the mixture resembles fine breadcrumbs. Use a round-bladed knife to stir in just enough cold water to make a soft (but not wet) dough. Turn out the dough onto a lightly floured surface and knead it gently and briefly until it is smooth and elastic. Wrap the dough in cling film or in a plastic bag and leave it in the fridge to 'rest' for 30 minutes.

When the pastry is ready to use, pre-heat the oven to 200°C/400°F/ Gas Mark 6, and place a baking tray in the oven to heat up. Grease a pie tin or dish about 22-26cms (9-10ins) in diameter. Roll out two-thirds of the pastry and use it to line the pie tin or dish.

Peel, quarter and core the apples, and cut them into thin or chunky slices as you prefer. Mix the apple pieces in a large bowl with the sugar, sift in the flour and cinnamon and mix well until the apple pieces are well coated. Mix in the sultanas if using. Turn the mixture into the pie tin or dish, heaping it up in the middle to form a mound. Sprinkle the lemon juice all over the filling, and dot small pieces of butter on the top. Brush round the pastry edge with some of the beaten egg. Roll out the rest of the pastry and use it to make a lid for the pie, trimming the edge. Press all round the edge of the pie with your thumb to seal the pastry edges well together. Cut two small crosses in the pastry lid with a sharp knife to allow steam to escape during cooking. Brush the lid of the pie with beaten egg, and sprinkle a little caster sugar over it.

Place the pie on the baking tray in the pre-heated oven (this helps the pastry base of the pie to cook through). Cook for 15 minutes, then reduce the heat to 190°C/375°F/Gas Mark 5 and cook for a further 25-30 minutes, or until the pastry is crisp and golden. Remove from the oven and sprinkle some extra sugar over the top whilst the pie is still hot. Leave the pie to 'rest' for 10 minutes before serving.

# RECIPE

## Hampshire Picnic Cake

The mixture of spices and honey in this cake gives it a lovely flavour.

115g/4oz butter or margarine, softened to room temperature
225g/8oz caster sugar or soft brown sugar
3 eggs, beaten
175g/6oz self-raising flour
¼ teaspoonful salt
½ teaspoonful ground nutmeg
½ teaspoonful ground cinnamon
2 tablespoonfuls milk
2 tablespoonfuls runny honey
¼ teaspoonful bicarbonate of soda
175g/6oz raisins or sultanas
175g/6oz chopped walnuts
6-8 walnut halves, to decorate

Pre-heat the oven to 160°C/325°F/Gas Mark 3 (slightly less for a fan oven). Grease and line a 900g (2 lb) loaf tin.

Sift the flour, salt and spices together into a bowl. In a separate bowl, cream together the butter or margarine and sugar until light and fluffy. Beat in a little of the beaten eggs and then some of the flour mixture. Repeat alternately until all is used up. Warm the milk very slightly in a pan, add the honey, then sprinkle in the bicarbonate of soda, stir until dissolved and add to the cake mixture. Add the chopped walnuts and dried fruit, and combine it all together well. Turn the mixture into the cake tin and bake just below the centre of the pre-heated oven for 1-1¼ hours, then lightly press the walnut halves into the top of the cake and bake for a further 40-45 minutes. Cover the top of the cake with kitchen foil if it seems to be browning too quickly. Leave the cake to cool in the tin before turning out on a wire rack and leaving to cool completely. Serve cut into slices.

The cake on the opposite page has quite a dense texture that keeps together well. This makes it ideal to include in a lunch box or a picnic, perhaps to take on a boating trip such as that being enjoyed by the people in this view on the Basingstoke Canal in 1908. Opened in 1794, this 37-mile-long waterway linked Basingstoke with London via its junction with the River Wey navigation at West Byfleet. It was built with the intention of boosting local trade by providing cheap transport for agricultural goods and locally produced timber, bricks and chalk, but the canal's construction costs were twice the estimate, and it was never commercially viable. The last commercial craft on the canal operated in 1950, and it then became derelict. The Surrey and Hampshire Canal Society was formed in 1966 to campaign for the canal's restoration and public ownership. This goal was achieved when Surrey and Hampshire County Councils purchased it in 1974, and restoration work began in earnest. It was officially reopened in 1991, and the canal is again navigable from Greywell Tunnel near Odiham to the River Wey.

**FLEET, BOATING ON THE BASINGSTOKE CANAL 1908** 60081x

# RECIPE

## GYPSY BREAD

This recipe is for a rich, dark, fruited tea-bread that is flavoured with black treacle. A tip for measuring the treacle is to put the empty saucepan on the weighing scales, turn the weight register back to '0' and then pour the required amount of the treacle into it until the weight reads 115g/4oz – and if you stand the treacle tin in a bowl of hot water before doing this, it will make the treacle runny and easier to pour. Be careful not to over-bake this cake, or it will turn out very dry and hard.

225g/8oz self-raising flour
A pinch of salt
½ teaspoonful mixed spice
½ teaspoonful ground ginger
115g/4oz soft brown sugar
115g/4oz sultanas
50g/2oz chopped mixed peel
(or replace the peel with the same weight of extra sultanas, if you prefer)
115g/4oz black treacle (see weighing tip above)
150ml/ ¼ pint milk
1 egg, beaten
½ teaspoonful bicarbonate of soda

Pre-heat the oven to 180°C/350°F/Gas Mark 4 and grease a 900g/2 lb loaf tin. Sift the flour into a large mixing bowl with the salt and spices. Stir in the sugar, sultanas and peel. Put the treacle in a saucepan, add all but one tablespoonful of the milk and gently warm it over a low heat, stirring, until the treacle is smooth and runny and the mixture is blended. Remove from the heat and leave to cool for a few minutes. Dissolve the bicarbonate of soda in the rest of the milk, mix it into the treacle liquid, then blend in the beaten egg. Pour into the flour mixture and mix well. Turn the mixture into the loaf tin and smooth the surface. Bake just below the centre of the pre-heated oven for 45–50 minutes, until the cake is risen and firm to the touch. Leave the cake to settle in the tin for 15 minutes before turning it out onto a wire rack to cool. When completely cool, store in an airtight container and leave until the next day before eating, when the hard outer crust of the cake will have softened. Serve cut into slices, spread with butter.

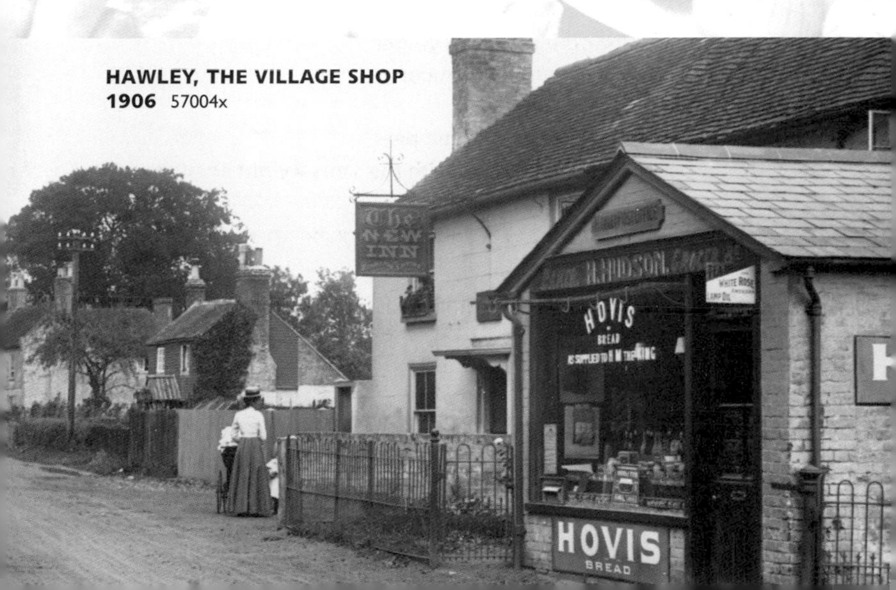


**HAWLEY, THE VILLAGE SHOP**
**1906** 57004x

# RECIPE

## Hampshire Drops

These small, domed biscuits can either be eaten as they are, or sandwiched together with a little raspberry or strawberry jam, or perhaps some butter icing made by beating icing sugar into softened butter, in a proportion of one part of butter to two parts of icing sugar, plus a little milk, and a few drops of vanilla extract if liked. This amount should make about 30 biscuits.

115g/4oz butter or margarine, softened to room temperature
115g/4oz caster sugar
1 egg, beaten
115g/4oz plain flour
115g/4oz cornflour
1 level teaspoonful baking powder
A little jam or butter icing (optional)

Pre-heat the oven to 190°C/375°F/Gas Mark 5 and grease a baking sheet.

Sift together the flour, cornflour and baking powder. In a separate bowl, cream together the butter or margarine and sugar until light and fluffy. Beat in the egg, a little at a time. Add the flour mixture, and mix together well to form a soft dough.

Flour your hands. Take rounded teaspoonfuls of dough and roll them in your hands to form small balls about the size of a cherry tomato. Place the balls on the baking tray, spaced well apart to allow them room to spread during cooking, and bake in the pre-heated oven for 10-12 minutes, until they are risen and firm to the touch, but not over-browned. Leave on the baking tray to cool and firm up for a few minutes, then cool on a wire tray.

LIPHOOK, CHILDREN AT THE SHOP 1911 63116x

# FRANCIS FRITH

## PIONEER VICTORIAN PHOTOGRAPHER

Francis Frith, founder of the world-famous photographic archive, was a complex and multi-talented man. A devout Quaker and a highly successful Victorian businessman, he was philosophical by nature and pioneering in outlook. By 1855 he had already established a wholesale grocery business in Liverpool, and sold it for the astonishing sum of £200,000, which is the equivalent today of over £15,000,000. Now in his thirties, and captivated by the new science of photography, Frith set out on a series of pioneering journeys up the Nile and to the Near East.

### INTRIGUE AND EXPLORATION

He was the first photographer to venture beyond the sixth cataract of the Nile. Africa was still the mysterious 'Dark Continent', and Stanley and Livingstone's historic meeting was a decade into the future. The conditions for picture taking confound belief. He laboured for hours in his wicker dark-room in the sweltering heat of the desert, while the volatile chemicals fizzed dangerously in their trays. Back in London he exhibited his photographs and was 'rapturously cheered' by members of the Royal Society. His reputation as a photographer was made overnight.

### VENTURE OF A LIFE-TIME

By the 1870s the railways had threaded their way across the country, and Bank Holidays and half-day Saturdays had been made obligatory by Act of Parliament. All of a sudden the working man and his family were able to enjoy days out, take holidays, and see a little more of the world.

With typical business acumen, Francis Frith foresaw that these new tourists would enjoy having souvenirs to commemorate their days out. For the next thirty years he travelled the country by train and by pony and trap, producing fine photographs of seaside resorts and beauty spots that were keenly bought by millions of Victorians. These prints were painstakingly pasted into family albums and pored over during the dark nights of winter, rekindling precious memories of summer excursions. Frith's studio was soon supplying retail shops all over the country, and by 1890 F Frith & Co had become the greatest specialist photographic publishing company in the world, with over 2,000 sales outlets, and pioneered the picture postcard.

## FRANCIS FRITH'S LEGACY

Francis Frith had died in 1898 at his villa in Cannes, his great project still growing. By 1970 the archive he created contained over a third of a million pictures showing 7,000 British towns and villages.

Frith's legacy to us today is of immense significance and value, for the magnificent archive of evocative photographs he created provides a unique record of change in the cities, towns and villages throughout Britain over a century and more. Frith and his fellow studio photographers revisited locations many times down the years to update their views, compiling for us an enthralling and colourful pageant of British life and character.

We are fortunate that Frith was dedicated to recording the minutiae of everyday life. For it is this sheer wealth of visual data, the painstaking chronicle of changes in dress, transport, street layouts, buildings, housing and landscape that captivates us so much today, offering us a powerful link with the past and with the lives of our ancestors.

Computers have now made it possible for Frith's many thousands of images to be accessed almost instantly. The archive offers every one of us an opportunity to examine the places where we and our families have lived and worked down the years. Its images, depicting our shared past, are now bringing pleasure and enlightenment to millions around the world a century and more after his death.

For further information visit: www.francisfrith.com

## Interior Decoration

Frith's photographs can be seen framed and as giant wall murals in thousands of pubs, restaurants, hotels, banks, retail stores and other public buildings throughout Britain. These provide interesting and attractive décor, generating strong local interest and acting as a powerful reminder of gentler days in our increasingly busy and frenetic world.

## Frith Products

All Frith photographs are available as prints and posters in a variety of different sizes and styles. In the UK we also offer a range of other gift and stationery products illustrated with Frith photographs, although many of these are not available for delivery outside the UK – see our web site for more information on the products available for delivery in your country.

## The Internet

Over 100,000 photographs of Britain can be viewed and purchased on the Frith web site. The web site also includes memories and reminiscences contributed by our customers, who have personal knowledge of localities and of the people and properties depicted in Frith photographs. If you wish to learn more about a specific town or village you may find these reminiscences fascinating to browse. Why not add your own comments if you think they would be of interest to others? See **www.francisfrith.com**

## PLEASE HELP US BRING FRITH'S PHOTOGRAPHS TO LIFE

Our authors do their best to recount the history of the places they write about. They give insights into how particular towns and villages developed, they describe the architecture of streets and buildings, and they discuss the lives of famous people who lived there. But however knowledgeable our authors are, the story they tell is necessarily incomplete.

Frith's photographs are so much more than plain historical documents. They are living proofs of the flow of human life down the generations. They show real people at real moments in history; and each of those people is the son or daughter of someone, the brother or sister, aunt or uncle, grandfather or grandmother of someone else. All of them lived, worked and played in the streets depicted in Frith's photographs.

We would be grateful if you would give us your insights into the places shown in our photographs: the streets and buildings, the shops, businesses and industries. Post your memories of life in those streets on the Frith website: what it was like growing up there, who ran the local shop and what shopping was like years ago; if your workplace is shown tell us about your working day and what the building is used for now. Read other visitors' memories and reconnect with your shared local history and heritage. With your help more and more Frith photographs can be brought to life, and vital memories preserved for posterity, and for the benefit of historians in the future.

Wherever possible, we will try to include some of your comments in future editions of our books. Moreover, if you spot errors in dates, titles or other facts, please let us know, because our archive records are not always completely accurate—they rely on 140 years of human endeavour and hand-compiled records. You can email us using the contact form on the website.

Thank you!

For further information, trade, or author enquiries please contact us at the address below:

**The Francis Frith Collection, 6 Oakley Business Park, Wylye Road, Dinton, Wiltshire SP3 5EU England.**

Tel: +44 (0)1722 716 376 Fax: +44 (0)1722 716 881

e-mail: sales@francisfrith.co.uk **www.francisfrith.com**